Dear Caroline,

I so had fun
picking out this
book especially for
you on your special
5th Grade graduation

Hugs,
Grammy

The Passion of Chocolate

by
Patrick Caton

Cover Photo © Thomas Lindley/FPG International
Cover Design and Typography by Roy Honegger

Published by Great Quotations Publishing Co.,
Glendale Heights, IL

Library of Congress Catalog Card
Number: 96-76127

ISBN 1-56245-272-X

Printed in Hong Kong

Chocolate—the word itself makes your mouth water. This book contains interesting information about chocolate—from its ancient discovery to how different varieties are made, and tempting recipes. Any way you look at it (or taste it), you'll feel *The Passion of Chocolate*.

Dedicated to:
Homer, Will, Remy, Tom, Paul,
Rod, Mosi, Matt, Jim, Larry,
Dan, Hutch and Dixie and
the Seven Dwarfs.

Table of Contents

The History of Chocolate......6

How Chocolate is Made.......10

Chocolate Dessert Recipes.....14

Chocolate Drink Recipes.......50

Chocolate Trivia.................55

Chocolate Quotes...............57

The History of Chocolate

Chocolate is made from the seeds of a tropical tree called the *cacao*. It was first cultivated by the Maya and Inca Indians in Central and South America. The exact date of its discovery is unclear, but it was used by these indigenous peoples centuries before the Spanish arrived in America.

The cacao tree is believed to have originated in the Amazon-Orinoco river basins in South America, and problems with commercial growing has scientists looking for original types of these trees in the region.

The Aztecs believe that one of their prophets brought the seeds back with him from paradise and sowed them in his garden. Upon eating the fruit of the trees, he was given universal wisdom and knowledge.

The beans were the base for two popular drinks in pre-Columbian Central America, *cacaoquahitl* and *chocolatl*. Both were commonly consumed by the Aztec elite. Spaniards reported that Aztec emperor Montezuma drank more than 50 cups of cacaoquahitl per day, a bitter brew made by boiling the dried and roasted beans in water. The Spaniards were more fond of chocolatl, a thicker brew of chocolate sweetened with honey and flavored with vanilla and other spices.

The first beans were brought to Europe in 1528 by Hernando Cortes. A closely guarded secret in Spain for nearly a century, it was first introduced in Italy in 1606, and it soon found its way across the continent. By the 1700's, cocoa had become a fashionable drink in London. The drink finally made its way to the United States later in the 18th century.

Chocolate, in its present-day form, began to take shape in 1828, when a process was developed in Holland by pressing cocoa butter from the ground and roasted beans, to make powdered chocolate. In 1848, "edible chocolate" was produced in England by combining cocoa butter with chocolate liquor and sugar. And milk chocolate was developed in 1876 by Daniel Peter, a Swiss, by adding milk solids to chocolate liquor.

How Chocolate is Made

Seed pods from cacao tree flowers are gathered and cut in two by a machete. The pods are filled with a whitish, sweet material that holds 30 to 40 seeds. After drying for 24 hours, the seeds in the pulp are stored in boxes and fermented. This fermentation process kills the seed, reduces bitterness, develops flavor and reddens the beans. The beans are now ready for cleaning and roasting, which reduces acidity and moisture content, and helps develop flavor. The beans are de-hulled, cracked and winnowed to make *nibs*. (To extract the benefit of the untreated cocoa bean, these cocoa nibs can be steeped in boiling water and made into a wholesome beverage.) Nibs from other plantations are combined to make different blends, then are put into heated grinders. These heated grinders reduce the nibs to an oily liquid called chocolate liquor. From this point the chocolate liquor can be processed into cocoa or chocolate. For cocoa, the liquor is pressed to remove a specific amount of cocoa butter. Cocoa sold in the U.S.

contains 11-22 % cocoa butter, while Great Britain's standard is a minimum of 20%. This is then pulverized and sifted. If your cocoa has been *dutched*, this means it has been treated with an alkalai solution to reduce acidity, mellow the flavor and darken the color. Chocolate, on the other hand, has cocoa butter added to the liquor. It is then *conched*, a process that aerates, emulsifies and develops further flavor in the chocolate. This takes from 4 to 72 hours. Then the chocolate is poured into bars or squares and cooled. This is called baking or plain chocolate.

Two popular types of chocolate are *sweet* and *milk*. Sweet chocolate contains chocolate liquor, sugar, added cocoa butter and other flavorings, such as vanilla, salt, cinnamon, etc. Milk chocolate is sweet chocolate with milk or milk solids added to the mix.

Cocoa and chocolate should be kept cool and dry. Excessive heat causes "fat bloom", characterized by a gray or white color. Too much moisture could lead to mold, a musty taste or *sugar bloom*, which causes the sugar in it to crystallize on the surface.

Chocolate Dessert Recipes

Fudge Brownie Frosting

3 T. butter, softened
3 T. cocoa
1 c. powdered sugar
1 to 2 T. milk
3/4 t. vanilla extract

In small mixer bowl, beat
butter and cocoa until blended.
Add powdered sugar, alternating with milk until spreading
consistency is reached.
Stir in vanilla.

Chocolate Icing

2 squares unsweetened
   baking chocolate
1/4 c. butter, softened
2 c. powdered sugar
1 t. vanilla extract
3 T. milk or light cream

In top of double boiler over
hot, not boiling, water melt
chocolate. In small mixer bowl,
beat butter until creamy.
Gradually add powdered sugar
and vanilla, beating until
blended. Add chocolate; beat
well. Add milk, beating until
spreading consistent.

Yield: about 1 1/3 cups

Creole Icing

3 T. butter, softened
3 1/4 c. powdered sugar
3 T. cocoa
Dash ground cinnamon
1/4 c. warm brewed coffee
1 T. warm water
1/2 t. vanilla extract

In small mixer bowl, beat butter until creamy. Add powdered sugar, cocoa and cinnamon alternately with coffee, water and vanilla; beat until spreading is consistent. (Add additional water, 1 teaspoon at a time, if necessary.)

Yield: about 1 3/4 cups

Chocolate Caramel Sauce

1/4 c. chocolate syrup
2 T. milk
1 T. butter
10 light caramels, unwrapped

In small saucepan, combine
syrup, milk, butter and
caramels. Cook over low heat,
stirring constantly, until mixture is smooth. Serve warm
sauce over ice cream.

Yield: about 2/3 cup

Cocoa Chocolate Sauce

1/4 c. butter
2 squares (2 oz.) unsweetened
  baking chocolate
3/4 c. sugar
2 T. cocoa
1/2 c. light cream
1 t. vanilla extract

In top of double boiler over
hot, not boiling, water melt
butter and chocolate. Stir in
sugar and cocoa; cook 5 minutes, stirring occasionally. Stir
in light cream and vanilla;
cook, stirring constantly, until
well blended. Serve warm
sauce over ice cream or cake.
Yield: about 1 cup

Flaherty's Campground S'Mores

Graham crackers
Marshmallows
Hershey Milk Chocolate bars

(NOTE: This recipe has no
exact measurements. Once you
have these basic ingredients,
you can really be creative.)
Place Hershey bar on graham
cracker. Roast marshmallow
over open flame. Once melted,
put marshmallow on choco-
late/graham cracker and lay
another graham cracker on top.
Press together. Eat it now!

Yield: good memories

Old Fashioned Chocolate Cake

4 1/2 squares unsweetened
  baking chocolate
1/2 c. water
3/4 c. butter, softened
2 1/4 c. sugar
6 eggs, separated
1 1/2 t. vanilla extract
2 2/3 c. cake flour
3 t. baking powder
3/4 t. salt
3/4 c. milk

Heat oven to 350°F. Grease and
flour 13 x 9 baking pan. In top
of double boiler over hot, not
boiling, water melt chocolate
with water. Set aside to cool
slightly. In large mixer bowl,

beat butter and sugar until
light and fluffy. Add egg yolks
and vanilla; beat well. Add
chocolate; beat until blended.
Stir together flour, baking powder and salt; add alternately
with milk to butter batter into
prepared pan. Bake 45 to 50
minutes or until wooden pick
inserted in center comes out
clean. Cool in pan on wire rack.
Frost as desired.

Yield: 12 to 15 servings

Chicago Fudge Cake

4 squares unsweetened
  baking chocolate
1 c. butter, softened
2 1/4 c. sugar
5 eggs, separated
2 3/4 c. cake flour
1 t. baking soda
1/2 t. baking powder
1/2 t. salt
1 1/2 c. buttermilk
1 t. vanilla extract

Heat oven to 350°F. Grease and
flour three 9-inch round baking
pans. In top of double boiler
over hot, not boiling, water
melt chocolate. Set aside to

cool slightly. In large mixer bowl, beat butter and sugar until light and fluffy. Add chocolate; beat until blended. Add egg yolks; beat well. Stir together flour baking soda, baking powder and salt; add alternately with buttermilk until stiff, but not dry; fold into batter. Pour batter into prepared pans. Bake 30 to 35 minutes or until wooden pick inserted in center comes out clean. Cool 10 minutes; remove from pans to wire racks. Cool completely before icing. Best with vanilla icing.

Yield: 10 to 12 servings

Upside Down Chocolate Cake

2 T. plus 1/3 c. butter
1/2 c. packed light
   brown sugar
1 can (1 lb.) apricot halves,
   drained
8 to 10 maraschino cherries,
   halved
3/4 c. granulated sugar
1/4 c. cocoa
Dash ground cinnamon
2 eggs
1 3/4 c. cake flour
1 t. baking soda
3/4 c. milk
1/2 t. vanilla extract

Heat oven to 350°F. In 9-inch
square pan, melt 2 T. butter in

oven. Remove. Stir in brown sugar. Arrange apricot halves, rounded side down, and cherries in the pan. Set aside. In small bowl, beat 1/3 c. butter and granulated sugar until light and fluffy. Add cocoa and cinnamon; beat until blended. Add eggs; beat well. Mix flour and baking soda; add alternating with milk to cocoa mixture, beating until well blended. Stir in vanilla. Pour batter into pan over fruit. Bake 45 to 50 minutes or until wooden pick inserted in center comes out clean. With metal spatula, loosen sides; invert cake onto serving plate. Serve warm. Yield: 8 servings

Chocolate Cream Pie

9-inch baked pastry shell
2 1/2 c. milk, divided
3 squares unsweetened baking
   chocolate, broken into pieces
1 c. sugar
3 T. all-purpose flour
3 T. cornstarch
1/2 t. salt
4 egg yolks, slightly beaten
2 T. butter
1 1/2 t. vanilla extract

Prepare pastry shell; cool. In
medium saucepan, combine
2 c. milk and chocolate. Cook
over low heat, stirring occasionally, until chocolate is
melted. In medium bowl, stir

together flour, cornstarch, sugar and salt. Gradually add remaining 1/2 c. milk, stirring until smooth; stir into chocolate mixture. Cook over medium heat, stirring constantly, until mixture is thickened and bubbly. Remove from heat; gradually add about 1 c. hot mixture to egg yolks. Return all to saucepan; bring to gentle boil. Cook and stir 2 minutes. Remove from heat; stir in butter and vanilla. Pour into pastry shell. Press plastic wrap directly onto surface. Cool; refrigerate until firm.

Yield: 8 servings

Our Gal Sundae Pie

9-inch baked pastry shell
2/3 c. packed light
   brown sugar
3 T. all-purpose flour
2 T. cornstarch
1/2 t. salt
1/2 c. (5.5 oz.) chocolate syrup
2 1/4 c. milk
3 egg yolks, well beaten
2 T. butter
1 t. vanilla extract
Optional:
   Maraschino cherries
   Sweetened whipped cream
   Milk chocolate bar,
   broken into pieces

Prepare pastry shell. In medium saucepan, stir together brown sugar, flour, cornstarch and salt. Gradually stir in milk, syrup and egg yolks. Cook over medium heat; stir in butter and vanilla. Pour into prepared crust; place plastic wrap directly on surface. Cool; refrigerate. Garnish with whipped cream, maraschino cherries and chocolate bar squares, if desired. For an added effect, try different flavored crusts.

Yield: 8 servings

Old Fashioned Chocolate Ice Cream

3 envelopes unflavored gelatin
1/2 c. cold water
1 c. whole milk
3/4 c. sugar
Dash salt
1 1/2 c. (1 lb.) chocolate syrup
2 c. (1 pt.) light cream
2 c. (1 pt.) whipping cream
2 T. vanilla extract

In medium saucepan, sprinkle gelatin over water; let stand 5 minutes. Add milk and sugar. Cook over low heat, stirring constantly, until gelatin is completely dissolved. Remove from heat; add salt and syrup,

stirring until well blended.
Cool. Refrigerate until cold.
Stir together chocolate mixture,
light cream, whipping cream
and vanilla; pour into 5-quart
ice cream freezer container.
Freeze according to manufacturer's directions.

Yield: about 4 quarts ice cream

Cocoa Marble Gingerbread

1/2 c. shortening
1 c. sugar
1 c. light molasses
2 eggs
1 t. baking soda
1 c. boiling water
2 c. all-purpose flour
1 t. salt
1/4 c. cocoa
1/2 t. ground cinnamon
1/2 t. ground ginger
1/4 t. ground cloves
1/4 t. ground nutmeg
Optional:
  Sweetened whipped cream

Heat oven to 350°F. Grease and
flour 13 x 9 pan. In large mixing

bowl, beat shortening, sugar
and molasses until blended;
blend in eggs. Stir baking soda
into boiling water to dissolve;
add to shortening mixture alternating with combined flour and
salt. Remove 2 c. batter to medium bowl; add cocoa, blending
well. Add spices to remaining
batter in large mixing bowl.
Alternately spoon batters into
prepared pan; with narrow spatula or knife, swirl gently
through batter to marble. Bake
40 to 45 minutes or until tooth-
pick inserted in center comes
out clean. Cut into squares.
Serve warm or cool with
whipped cream, if desired.
Yield: about 12 servings

Chocolate Marshmallow Pudding

3 c. milk
1/2 c. (5.5 oz.) chocolate syrup
1/4 c. sugar
3 T. all-purpose flour
Dash salt
1 egg
1 t. vanilla extract
1 c. miniature marshmallows

Heat oven to 400°F. In medium saucepan, stir milk and syrup. Cook over medium heat until tiny bubbles form at edges of pan. In medium bowl, stir together sugar, flour, salt and egg. Stir half of the hot milk mixture into sugar mixture.

Return all to saucepan; cook, stirring constantly, until mixture just begins to boil. Reduce heat; cook and stir 2 minutes. Remove from heat; stir in vanilla. Pour mixture into 1 1/2 quart baking dish; top with marshmallows. Place in oven until marshmallows are lightly browned, about 5 minutes. Cool; refrigerate. Serve cold.

Yield: about 12 servings

Quick Creamy Chocolate Pudding

2/3 c. sugar
1/4 c. cocoa
3 T. cornstarch
1/4 t. salt
2 1/4 c. milk
2 T. butter
1 t. vanilla extract
Optional:
  Sweetened whipped cream
  Chopped nuts

In medium saucepan, stir together sugar, cocoa, cornstarch and salt; gradually stir in milk. Cook over medium heat, stirring constantly, until mixture boils; boil and stir 1

minute. Remove from heat; stir
in butter and vanilla. Pour into
individual serving dishes.
Press wax paper directly onto
surface. Refrigerate. Garnish
with whipped cream and nuts,
if desired.

Yield: 4 to 5 servings

Chocolate Soufflé

2 envelopes unflavored gelatin
2/3 c. sugar
1/3 c. cocoa
2 1/4 c. milk
3 egg yolks, beaten
3/4 t. vanilla extract
1 1/2 c. cold whipping cream

Measure length of aluminum foil to fit around 1-quart souffle dish; fold in thirds lengthwise. Lightly oil one side of collar; tape securely to outside of dish, oiled side in, allowing collar to extend 3 inches above rim of dish. Set aside. In medium saucepan, stir together gelatin, sugar and cocoa; stir in milk and egg yolks. Let stand 2 minutes. Cook over low heat, stirring constantly, until gelatin is completely dissolved. Remove from heat; stir in mixture mounds slightly when dropped from spoon. In small mixer bowl, beat whipping cream until stiff; fold into chocolate mixture. Pour into prepared dish; refrigerate 4 to 6 hours or until set. Just before serving, carefully remove foil.

Yield: 6 to 8 servings

Chocolate Dessert Waffles

1/2 c. butter
2 squares unsweetened
  baking chocolate
3/4 c. sugar
1 t. vanilla extract
2 eggs
1 1/2 c. all-purpose flour
1 t. cream of tartar
1/2 t. baking soda
1/2 c. buttermilk
1 c. chopped nuts
Vanilla ice cream

In medium saucepan over low
heat, melt butter and chocolate.
Add sugar and vanilla; stir
until blended. Remove from

heat; add eggs, one at a time, beating after each addition until well blended. Stir together flour, cream of tartar and baking soda; add alternating with buttermilk to chocolate mixture. Stir in nuts. Bake in waffle iron according to manufacturer's directions. Carefully remove waffle from iron. (When first taken from waffle iron, the waffle will be soft, but will become crisp as it cools.) Serve warm with scoop of ice cream.

Chocolate Tea Bread

1/4 c. butter, softened
2/3 c. sugar
1 egg
1 1/2 c. all-purpose flour
1/3 c. cocoa
1 t. baking soda
1/4 t. salt
1 c. buttermilk
1/2 c. dairy sour cream
3/4 c. chopped nuts
3/4 c. raisins

Heat oven to 350°F. Grease
8 x 4 loaf pan. In large mixer
bowl, beat butter until creamy.
Gradually add sugar, beating
until well blended. Add egg;

beat well. Stir together flour, cocoa, baking soda and salt; add alternately with buttermilk to butter mixture. Stir in sour cream. Add nuts and raisins; stir until blended. Pour batter into prepared pan. Bake 1 hour and 15 to 20 minutes or until wooden pick inserted into center comes out clean. Cool 10 minutes; remove from pan to wire rack. Cool completely. Serve with softened cream cheese, if desired.

Yield: 1 loaf

Chocolate Chip Cookies

3/4 c. butter, softened
1 c. packed light brown sugar
1/2 c. granulated sugar
1 t. vanilla extract
2 eggs
2 c. all-purpose flour
1 t. baking soda
1 t. salt
2 c. (12 oz. pkg.) semi-sweet
   chocolate chips

Heat oven to 375°F. In large mixer bowl, beat butter, brown sugar, granulated sugar and vanilla until light and fluffy. Add eggs; beat well. Stir together flour, baking soda and salt; gradually add to butter mixture, beating until blended. Stir in chocolate chips. Drop by teaspoonfuls onto ungreased cookie sheet. Bake 8 to 10 minutes or until lightly browned. Remove from cookie sheet to wire rack. Cool completely.

Yield: about 7 dozen cookies

Chocolate Brownies

1/2 c. butter, softened
1 c. sugar
2 eggs
1 t. vanilla extract
1 1/4 c. all-purpose flour
1/4 c. cocoa
1/4 t. baking soda
3/4 c. chocolate syrup
Optional:
  1 c. peanut butter chips

Heat oven to 350°F. Grease
13 x 9 pan. In large mixer
bowl, beat butter, sugar, eggs
and vanilla until light and
fluffy. Stir together flour, cocoa
and baking soda; add alternating

with syrup to butter mixture. Stir in peanut butter chips, if desired. Pour batter into prepared pan. Bake 40 to 45 minutes or until brownies begin to pull away from the sides of the pan. Cool completely in pan on wire rack. Cut into squares. Try using Fudge Brownie Frosting!

Yield: about 24 brownies

Angel Fudge

2 c. sugar
1 c. milk
1 c. chocolate syrup
1 T. butter
1 t. vanilla extract
3/4 c. marshmallow creme

Butter 8-inch square pan. In
heavy 3-quart saucepan, combine sugar, milk and syrup.
Cook over medium heat, stirring constantly, until well
blended. Continue to cook,
without stirring, to 234°F or
until syrup, when dripped into
very cold water, forms a soft
ball which flattens when

removed from water. (Bulb of candy thermometer should not rest on bottom of saucepan.) Remove from heat. Add butter, vanilla and marshmallow creme. Do not stir. Cool at room temperature to 110°F (lukewarm). Beat with wooden spoon until fudge loses gloss (fudge will hold shape). Quickly spread into prepared pan; cool. Cut into squares.

Yield: about 3 dozen candies

Chocolate Drink Recipes

Rich Iced Chocolate

4 c. (1 qt.) water
1 c. sugar
4 squares unsweetened baker's
  chocolate, broken into pieces
Dash salt
1 t. vanilla extract
2 c. (1 pt.) cold whipping cream
Crushed ice
Optional:
  Whipped cream

In large saucepan, stir together
water and sugar; add chocolate
pieces and salt. Cook over medium heat, stirring occasionally.

Remove from heat; cool
completely. Stir in vanilla.
In large mixing bowl, beat 2
cups whipping cream until
slightly thickened. Add chocolate mixture; beat with rotary
beater or wire whisk until
slightly foamy. Fill glasses one-
half full with ice; add chocolate
mixture. Top with whipped
cream, if desired.

Yield: eight 8-oz. servings

Frosted Chocolate Shake

3/4 c. milk
2 to 3 T. chocolate syrup
1 t. sugar
1/2 t. vanilla extract
1/2 c. vanilla ice cream
Optional:
  Maraschino cherry

In blender, combine milk, syrup, sugar and vanilla; cover and blend. Add ice cream; cover and blend until smooth. Garnish with cherry, if desired. Serve immediately.

Hot Cocoa

3 T. sugar
2 T. cocoa
Dash salt
1/4 c. hot water
1 1/2 c. milk
Marshmallows or creme

In medium saucepan, combine
sugar, cocoa and salt; stir in
water. Cook over medium
heat, stirring constantly, until
boiling; boil 2 minutes. Add
milk. Heat to serving temperature, stirring occasionally.
Remove from heat; stir in vanilla. Beat with whisk until foamy.
Top with marshmallows.
Yield: three 6-oz. servings

Royal Hot Chocolate

2 squares unsweetened
  baking chocolate
1 can (14 oz.) sweetened
  condensed milk
4 cups boiling water
Dash salt
1 t. vanilla extract
Whipped cream
Ground cinnamon

In double boiler over hot, not
boiling, water melt chocolate.
Stir in condensed milk. Slowly
add water, stirring until well
blended. Stir in salt and vanilla. Top with whipped cream
and cinnamon, if desired.
Yield: eight 6-oz. servings

Chocolate Trivia:

• Cocoa can be substituted for unsweetened baking chocolate in many recipes. One table-spoon of shortening or oil must be added to each 3 tablespoons of cocoa.

• Use caution when storing chocolate. It can absorb the odors around it. (Like onion in a refrigerator)

• The word, "chocolate", derived from two Mayan words, meaning sour water.

• Bring out the flavor in soups and stews by adding a small amount of unsweetened chocolate or cocoa powder.

• When melting chocolate in a double boiler, don't let the top pan touch the water in the lower pan, or the chocolate may become grainy.

• About 70% of all candy bars are chocolate-coated.

• Chocolate is best kept in a cool (60° - 70°F), dry place. You should only refrigerate chocolate if it is in direct heat, direct sunlight or direct view during a chocolate attack.

Chocolate Quotes

"Research tells us that fourteen out of any ten individuals like chocolate."

—*Sandra Boynton*

"What food do you crave? Ask the question with enough smoldering emphasis on the last word, and the answer is bound to be chocolate."

—*Diane Ackerman*

"Flowers speak the language of love for some, but for others, it's chocolate that fans the flames."

—*Rebecca J. Pate*

"If you were to ask someone what he remembers about his first love, I think you'll find it will not be too different from how he describes chocolate."

—*James Switzer*

"Chocolate is not only pleasant of taste, but it is a veritable balm of the mouth, for the maintaining of all glands and humours in a good state of health. Thus it is, that all who drink it, possess a sweet breath."

—*Stephani Blancardi*
(1650 - 1702), Italian Physician

"Passion is made tangible in a single taste of chocolate."

—*Thomas Clary*

"The superiority of chocolate, both for health and nourishment, will soon give it the preference over tea and coffee in America as it has in Spain."

—*Thomas Jefferson*

Uno, dos, tres, cho-
Uno, dos, tres, -co-
Uno, dos, tres, -la-
Uno, dos, tres, -te
Bate, bate, chocolate.

—*Traditional Spanish rhyme*

"It's a sin, wickedly rich and fattening, but every spoonful is glory, and that's what chocolate mousse [should] be."

—*Julia Child*

"The divine drink, which builds up resistance and fights fatigue. A cup of this precious drink permits a man to walk for a whole day without food."

—*Montezuma*

"Like the final act of a play or the crescendo of a symphony, we expect a good chocolate sweet to leave us speechless, craving for more."

—*Suzanne Ausnit*

"…the best part of Easter is eating your children's candy while they are sleeping and trying to convince them the next morning that the chocolate rabbit came with one ear."

—*Anna Quindlen*

"Chocolate is heavenly, mellow, sensual, deep, dark, sumptuous, gratifying, potent, dense, creamy, seductive, suggestive, rich, excessive, silky, smooth, luxurious, celestial. Chocolate is downfall, happiness, pleasure, love, ecstasy, fantasy… chocolate makes us wicked, guilty, sinful, healthy, chic, happy."

—*Elaine Sherman*

"Chocolate makes otherwise normal people melt into strange states of ecstasy."

—*John West*

"The ladies of the New World, it seems, are mad for chocolate. We are told that, not content to drink it every moment of the day at home, they sometimes have it brought to them in church. This habit brought down on them the censure of their confessors, who ended up, however, in taking their part and sharing their chocolate."

—*Alexandre Dumas*

"Other things are just food. But chocolate's chocolate."

—*Patrick Skene Catling*